DO YOU BELIEVE?
STONEHENGE

by Natalie Deniston

pogo

Ideas for Parents and Teachers

Pogo Books let children practice reading informational text while introducing them to nonfiction features such as headings, labels, sidebars, maps, and diagrams, as well as a table of contents, glossary, and index.

Carefully leveled text with a strong photo match offers early fluent readers the support they need to succeed.

Before Reading

- "Walk" through the book and point out the various nonfiction features. Ask the student what purpose each feature serves.
- Look at the glossary together. Read and discuss the words.

Read the Book

- Have the child read the book independently.
- Invite him or her to list questions that arise from reading.

After Reading

- Discuss the child's questions. Talk about how he or she might find answers to those questions.
- Prompt the child to think more. Ask: Who do you think built Stonehenge? Why do you think they built it?

Pogo Books are published by Jump!
5357 Penn Avenue South
Minneapolis, MN 55419
www.jumplibrary.com

Copyright © 2025 Jump!
International copyright reserved in all countries. No part of this book may be reproduced in any form without written permission from the publisher.

Library of Congress Cataloging-in-Publication Data

Names: Deniston, Natalie, author.
Title: Stonehenge / by Natalie Deniston.
Description: Minneapolis, MN: Jump!, Inc., [2025]
Series: Do you believe? | Includes index.
Audience: Ages 7-10
Identifiers: LCCN 2024002613 (print)
LCCN 2024002614 (ebook)
ISBN 9798892132305 (hardcover)
ISBN 9798892132312 (paperback)
ISBN 9798892132329 (ebook)
Subjects: LCSH: Stonehenge (England)—Juvenile literature.
Classification: LCC DA142 .D46 2025 (print)
LCC DA142 (ebook)
DDC 936.2/31—dc23/eng/20240122
LC record available at https://lccn.loc.gov/2024002613
LC ebook record available at https://lccn.loc.gov/2024002614

Editor: Jenna Gleisner
Designer: Emma Almgren-Bersie

Photo Credits: Ahrys_Art/iStock, cover; jessicaphoto/iStock, 1; RollingEarth/iStock, 3; joaoccdj/Shutterstock, 4; Anita van den Broek/Shutterstock, 5; Susan Vineyard/iStock, 6-7; PTZ Pictures/Shutterstock, 8; Sergio Azenha/Alamy, 9; njaganath/iStock, 10-11; The Picture Art Collection/Alamy, 12-13 (foreground); Shutterstock, 12-13 (background); duncan1890/iStock, 14-15; Kirsty Wigglesworth/AP Images, 16; Chromatika Multimedia snc/Shutterstock, 17 (UFO); VitaliyPozdeyev/iStock, 17 (Stonehenge); AndyRoland/iStock, 18-19, 23; Alexey_Fedoren/iStock, 20-21.

Printed in the United States of America at Corporate Graphics in North Mankato, Minnesota.

TABLE OF CONTENTS

CHAPTER 1
Standing Stones...................4

CHAPTER 2
Mystery Builders................8

CHAPTER 3
What Is It For?..................16

QUICK FACTS & TOOLS
Timeline..............................22
Glossary..............................23
Index...................................24
To Learn More...................24

CHAPTER 1

STANDING STONES

The Sun rises over Salisbury **Plain** in England. It shines on giant stones. What is this place? It is Stonehenge.

Stonehenge is a **monument**. Large stone **pillars** stand in a circle. Some have stones on top.

CHAPTER 1 5

CHAPTER 1

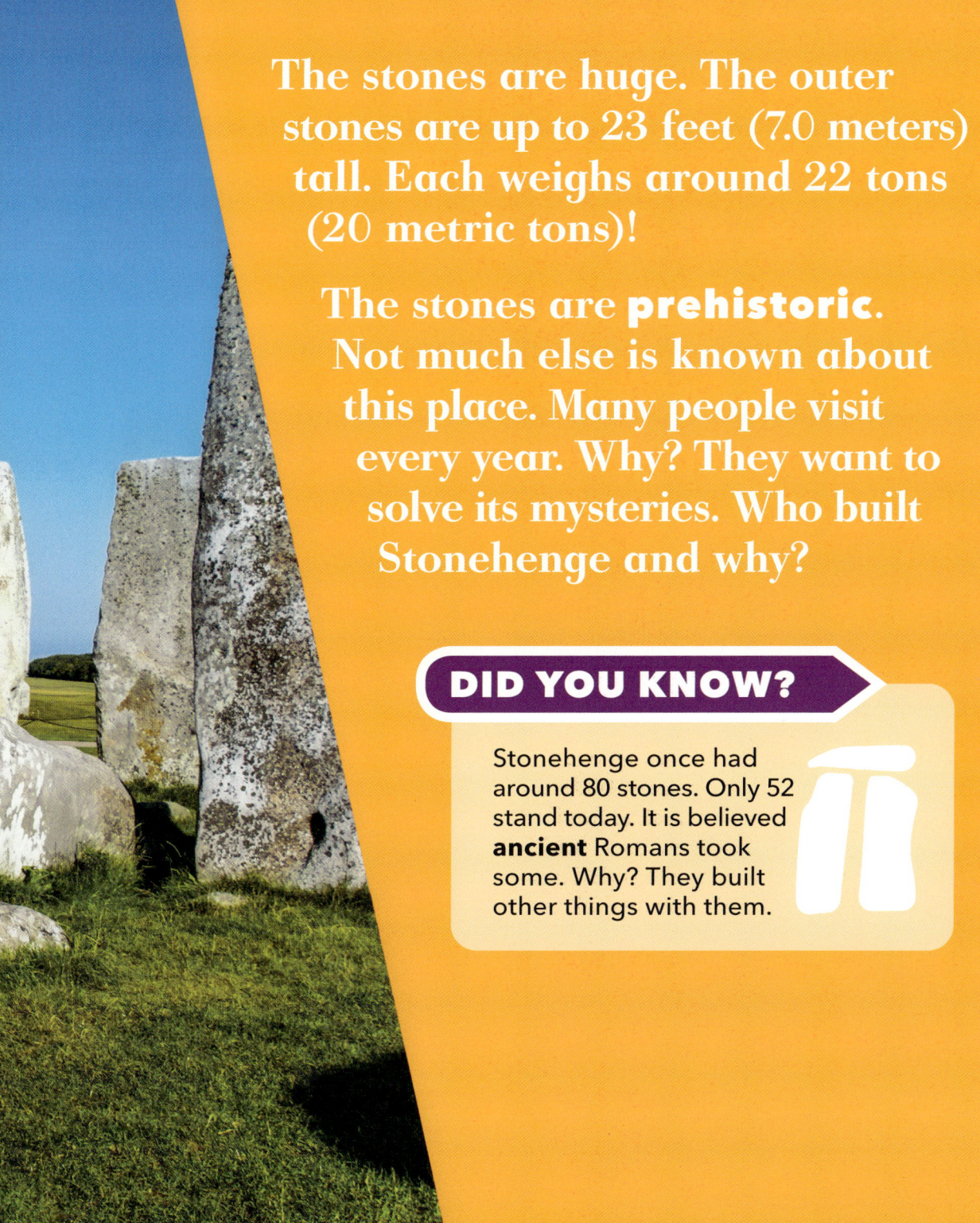

The stones are huge. The outer stones are up to 23 feet (7.0 meters) tall. Each weighs around 22 tons (20 metric tons)!

The stones are **prehistoric**. Not much else is known about this place. Many people visit every year. Why? They want to solve its mysteries. Who built Stonehenge and why?

DID YOU KNOW?

Stonehenge once had around 80 stones. Only 52 stand today. It is believed **ancient** Romans took some. Why? They built other things with them.

CHAPTER 2
MYSTERY BUILDERS

Scientists studied Stonehenge. What did they learn? The stones are from different times. This means Stonehenge was built in **stages**. It took thousands of years to build.

People started building it about 5,000 years ago. They dug a **ditch**. It is around a group of holes. They are called the Aubrey Holes. They are named after the man who found them. The holes are now filled in. They are marked.

CHAPTER 2   9

Over time, stones were added. Why? We don't know! Some stones came from more than 220 miles (354 kilometers) away. The largest came from about 20 miles (32 km) away. How did people move such large stones? Nobody knows. Maybe they used sleds and **rollers**.

TAKE A LOOK!

How far did the Stonehenge stones travel? Take a look!

CHAPTER 2

Who built Stonehenge? This is also a mystery. There are many **theories**. English **folklore** says Merlin the wizard moved the stones. Giants helped him. This story says the stones mark a large grave.

WHAT DO YOU THINK?

Some people believe **aliens** built Stonehenge. Why? They don't think humans could move such heavy stones. Who do you think moved them?

CHAPTER 2

giant

CHAPTER 2

Some believe druids built Stonehenge. Druids were religious leaders. They led the **Celts** of ancient Europe. But this is not likely. Why? The first known writing of druids is 2,400 years old. Stonehenge is much older.

> ### DID YOU KNOW?
> Some modern druids gather at Stonehenge for celebrations. There is a winter **solstice** and a summer solstice. On these days, druids celebrate the Sun.

CHAPTER 3
WHAT IS IT FOR?

We do not know who built Stonehenge. We also do not know why. Many people study it. They look for buried objects. These tell us more about Stonehenge.

Some say aliens built Stonehenge. They think it is a place to land spaceships. Why? There have been many **UFO** sightings here.

CHAPTER 3 17

Many graves have been found at Stonehenge. Maybe it was a cemetery. Or maybe it was a healing place. Sick or injured people may have traveled here. If they died, they might have been buried here.

The stones may have also been used in **rituals**. The Sun lines up with the stones on the summer and winter solstices. Because of this, some people believe it is a sort of calendar. Ancient people may have celebrated solstices here.

Stonehenge is a mystery. We know very little about it. Will we ever learn who built it and why? What do you believe?

WHAT DO YOU THINK?

More than 1 million people visit Stonehenge every year. Why do you think people visit? Would you like to? Why or why not?

CHAPTER 3

QUICK FACTS & TOOLS

TIMELINE

Stonehenge has existed for thousands of years. Take a look!

3000 BCE
A ditch and 56 holes are dug at Stonehenge.

2500 BCE
The first stones are placed in a circle.

2470-2280 BCE
The stones are rearranged. They now line up with the Sun on the summer and winter solstices.

2200 BCE
The stones are rearranged again. The outer stones are in a circle. The inner stones are in an oval.

1666
John Aubrey discovers holes at Stonehenge. They are later named the Aubrey Holes.

1918
The land Stonehenge is on is given to the British government. Everyone can now visit.

1986
Stonehenge is made a World Heritage Site. This honor is given to important historical places.

2024
People continue to study Stonehenge. They hope to find out who built it and why.

GLOSSARY

aliens: Creatures from other planets.

ancient: Very old or from the very distant past.

Celts: Ancient peoples who lived in Europe, including Great Britain and Ireland.

ditch: A long, narrow trench.

folklore: A group of people's stories, customs, and beliefs that are handed down from one generation to the next.

monument: A statue, building, or other structure that reminds people of an event or person.

pillars: Columns that support parts of buildings or stand as monuments.

plain: A large, flat area of land.

prehistoric: From a time before written history.

rituals: Acts that are always performed in the same way, often as part of religious or social ceremonies.

rollers: Cylinders or rods placed under objects to move them.

solstice: One of two times each year when one of Earth's two poles is farthest from the Sun.

stages: Steps or points in a process.

theories: Ideas or opinions that are based on some facts or evidence but are not proven.

UFO: Unidentified Flying Object. A UFO is any unknown object in the sky.

QUICK FACTS & TOOLS 23

INDEX

aliens 12, 17
ancient Romans 7
Aubrey Holes 9
calendar 19
Celts 14
ditch 9
druids 14
English folklore 12
giants 12
grave 12, 19
Merlin 12
rituals 19
Salisbury Plain, England 4
sleds and rollers 10
solstice 14, 19
stages 8
stones 4, 5, 7, 8, 10, 11, 12, 16, 19
studied 8, 16
Sun 4, 14, 19
visit 7, 20

TO LEARN MORE

Finding more information is as easy as 1, 2, 3.
1. Go to www.factsurfer.com
2. Enter "Stonehenge" into the search box.
3. Choose your book to see a list of websites.